Sweeney Astray

SEAMUS HEANEY

Sweeney Astray

faber and faber
LONDON · BOSTON

First published in Ireland in 1983
by Field Day Theatre Company, Derry
First published in London in 1984
Reprinted 1984
by Faber and Faber Limited
3 Queen Square London WC1N 3AU

Printed in Great Britain by
Whitstable Litho Ltd., Whitstable, Kent
All rights reserved

British Library Cataloguing in Publication Data

Heaney, Seamus
Sweeney astray.
1. Title
821'.914   OR6058.E2
ISBN 0-571-13360-6
ISBN 0-571-13303-7 Pbk

This version of *Buile Suibhne* is based on J. G. O'Keeffe's bilingual edition, which was published by the Irish Texts Society in 1913. In the meantime, Flann O'Brien gave its central character a second life, as hilarious as it was melancholy, when he made Sweeney part of the apparatus of his novel *At Swim-Two-Birds*; and a number of other poets and scholars have continued to make translations of different sections of the verse.

The basis of the 1913 edition is a manuscript written in County Sligo between 1671 and 1674. This manuscript is part of the Stowe collection in the Royal Irish Academy and O'Keeffe believed that, on linguistic grounds, "the text might have been composed at any time between the years 1200 and 1500." Nevertheless, the thing was already taking shape in the ninth century. O'Keeffe cites a reference in the *Book of Aicill*, a text dating from the tenth century at the latest, to stories and poems relating to Sweeney's madness; and other evidence from literary and historical sources leads him to conclude that the *Buile Suibhne* which we now possess is a development of traditions dating back to the time of the Battle of Moira (A.D. 637), the battle where Sweeney went mad and was transformed, in fulfilment of St. Ronan's curse, into a bird of the air.

What we have, then, is a literary creation; unlike Finn McCool or Cuchulain, Sweeney is not a given figure of myth or legend but an historically situated character, although the question of whether he is based upon an historical king called Sweeney has to remain an open one. But the literary imagination which fastened upon him as an image was clearly in the grip of a tension between the newly dominant Christian ethos and the older, re calcitrant Celtic temperament. The opening sections which recount the collision between the peremptory ecclesiastic and the sacral king, and the closing pages of uneasy reconciliation set in St. Moling's monastery, are the most explicit treatment of this recurrent theme. This alone makes the work a significant one, but it does not exhaust its significance. For example, insofar as Sweeney is also a figure of the artist, displaced, guilty, assuaging himself by his utterance, it is possible to read the work as an aspect of the quarrel between free creative imagination and the constraints of religious, political, and domestic obligation. It is equally possible, in a more opportunistic spirit, to dwell upon Sweeney's easy sense of cultural affinity with both western Scotland and southern Ireland as exemplary for all men and women in contemporary Ulster, or to ponder the thought that this Irish invention may well have been a development of a British original, vestigially present in the tale of the madman called Alan (Sections 46–50).

But the work makes its immediate claims more by its local power to affect us than by any general implications we may discover in its pattern. We have to go to *King Lear*, to Edgar's jabbering masquerade as poor Tom—itself an interesting parallel to Sweeney's condition—to find poetry as piercingly exposed to the beauties and severities of the natural world. We may even want to go back further, to the hard weather of the Anglo-Saxon "Seafarer," or, in order to match the occasional opposite moods of jubilation, to the praise poetry of the early Irish hermits. It was the bareness and durability of the writing here, its double note of relish and penitence, that first tempted me to try my hand at it and gave me the encouragement to persist with stretches of less purely inspired quatrains.

My first impulse had been to forage for the best lyric moments and to present them as poetic orphans, out of the context of the story. These points of poetic intensity, rather than the overall organization of the narrative, establish the work's highest artistic levels and offer the strongest invitations to the translator of verse. Yet I gradually felt I had to earn the right to do the high points by undertaking the whole thing: what I was dealing with, after all, is a major work in the canon of medieval literature.

Nevertheless, a small number of the original stanzas have been excluded (see Notes, page ix). I occasionally abbreviated the linking narrative and in places have used free verse to render the more heightened prose passages. O'Keeffe has been my guide to the interpretation of the line-by-line meaning, though I have now and again invested the poems with a more subjective tone than they possess in Irish. The stanza forms employed do not reflect the syllabic and assonantal disciplines of the original metres, but since the work could be regarded as a primer of lyric genres—laments, dialogues, litanies, rhapsodies, curses—I trust that the variety of dramatic pitch in the English will compensate to some extent for the loss of the metrical satisfactions in the Irish.

My fundamental relation with Sweeney, however, is topographical. His kingdom lay in what is now south County Antrim and north County Down, and for over thirty years I lived on the verges of that territory, in sight of some of Sweeney's places and in earshot of others—Slemish, Rasharkin, Benevenagh, Dunseverick, the Bann, the Roe, the Mournes. When I began work on this version, I had just moved to Wicklow, not all that far from Sweeney's final resting ground at St. Mullins. I was in a country of woods and hills and remembered that the green spirit of the hedges embodied in Sweeney had first been embodied for me in the persons of a family of tinkers, also called Sweeney, who used to camp in the ditchbacks along the road to the first school I attended. One way or another, he seemed to have been with me from the start.

S. H.

NOTES AND ACKNOWLEDGEMENTS

The sections of the text are numbered to correspond with J. G. O'Keeffe's divisions in the Irish Texts Society edition.

Six stanzas have been dropped from Section 16, seven from Section 40, and one from Section 43. In the first case, the material omitted is historical allusion; in the second, obscurity defeated ingenuity; and in the third, I felt that the English poem came to rest better at the penultimate stanza.

Section 82 and the first fifteen stanzas of Section 83 have also been excluded. There an exchange occurs between Moling, Mongan, and Sweeney which is essentially a recapitulation and seemed to me to impede the momentum of the conclusion.

I have anglicized the name of Sweeney's kingdom, Dal Araidhe, to Dal-Arie, and in dealing with other place names have followed the suggestions in O'Keeffe's notes and index. In the following cases, where no help was offered, I took the liberty of inventing my own equivalents of the Irish: Kilreagan, Cloonkill, Kilnoo, Drumfree, Drumduff, Kilsooney, Doovey, Creegaille, Glasgally.

I am grateful for various encouragements and assistances offered by Dr. Deirdre Flanagan, Henry Pearson, Colin Middleton, and Professor Brendan McHugh.

Sweeney Astray

We have already told how Sweeney, son of Colman Cuar and 1
king of Dal-Arie, went astray when he flew out of the battle.
This story tells the why and the wherefore of his fits and trips,
why he of all men was subject to such frenzies; and it also
tells what happened to him afterwards.

There was a certain Ronan Finn in Ireland, a holy and dis- 2
tinguished cleric. He was ascetic and pious, an active mission-
ary, a real Christian soldier. He was a worthy servant of God,
one who punished his body for the good of his soul, a shield
against vice and the devil's attacks, a gentle, genial, busy man.

One time when Sweeney was king of Dal-Arie, Ronan was 3
there marking out a church called Killaney. Sweeney was in
a place where he heard the clink of Ronan's bell as he was
marking out the site, so he asked his people what the sound
was.

—It is Ronan Finn, son of Bearach, they said. He is mark-
ing out a church in your territory and what you hear is the
ringing of his bell.

Sweeney was suddenly angered and rushed away to hunt
the cleric from the church. Eorann, his wife, a daughter of
Conn of Ciannacht, tried to hold him back and snatched at
the fringe of his crimson cloak, but the silver cloak-fastener
broke at the shoulder and sprang across the room. She got

the cloak all right but Sweeney had bolted, stark naked, and soon landed with Ronan.

4 He found the cleric glorifying the King of heaven and earth, in full voice in front of his psalter, a beautiful illuminated book. Sweeney grabbed the book and flung it into the cold depths of a lake nearby, where it sank without trace. Then he took hold of Ronan and was dragging him out through the church when he heard a cry of alarm. The call came from a servant of Congal Claon's who had come with orders from Congal to summon Sweeney to battle at Moira. He gave a full report of the business and Sweeney went off directly with the servant, leaving the cleric distressed at the loss of his psalter and smarting from such contempt and abuse.

5 A day and a night passed and then an otter rose out of the lake with the psalter and brought it to Ronan, completely unharmed. Ronan gave thanks to God for that miracle, and cursed Sweeney, saying:

6
> Sweeney has trespassed on me
> and abused me grievously
> and laid violent hands on me
> to drag me with him from Killarney.
>
> When Sweeney heard my bell ringing
> he came all of a sudden hurtling
> in terrible rage against me
> to drive me off and banish me.

Outrage like that, and eviction
from the first place I had chosen,
were too much for me to bear.
Therefore, God answered my prayer.

My hand was locked in Sweeney's hand
until he heard the loud command
to battle: Come away and join
arms with Donal on Moira's plain.

So I offered thanks and praise
for the merciful release,
that unhoped-for, timely summons
to arm and join the high prince.

From far off he approached the field
that drove his mind and senses wild.
He shall roam Ireland, mad and bare.
He shall find death on the point of a spear.

The psalter that he grabbed and tore
from me and cast into deep water—
Christ brought it back without a spot.
The psalter stayed immaculate.

A day and a night in brimming waters,
my speckled book was none the worse!
Through the will of God the Son
an otter gave me it again.

This psalter that he profaned
I bequeath with a malediction:
that it bode evil for Colman's race
the day this psalter meets their eyes.

Bare to the world, here came Sweeney
to harass and to harrow me:
therefore, it is God's decree
bare to the world he'll always be.

Eorann, daughter of Conn of Ciannacht,
tried to hold him by his cloak.
Eorann has my blessing for this
but Sweeney lives under my curse.

7 After that, Ronan came to Moira to make peace between
Donal, son of Aodh, and Congal Claon, son of Scannlan, but
he did not succeed. Nevertheless, the cleric's presence was
taken as a seal and guarantee of the rules of the battle; they
made agreements that no killing would be allowed except
between those hours they had set for beginning and ending
the fight each day. Sweeney, however, would continually
violate every peace and truce which the cleric had ratified,
slaying a man each day before the sides were engaged and
slaying another each evening when the combat was finished.
Then, on the day fixed for the great battle, Sweeney was in the
field before everyone else.

He was dressed like this:
next his white skin, the shimmer of silk;
and his satin girdle around him;
and his tunic, that reward of service
and gift of fealty from Congal,
was like this—
crimson, close-woven,
bordered in gemstones and gold,
a rustle of sashes and loops,
the studded silver gleaming,
the slashed hem embroidered in points.
He had an iron-shod spear in each hand,
a shield of mottled horn on his back,
a gold-hilted sword at his side.

He marched out like that until he encountered Ronan with eight psalmists from his community. They were blessing the armies, sprinkling them with holy water, and they sprinkled Sweeney with the rest. Sweeney thought they had done it just to mock him, so he lifted one of his spears, hurled it, and killed one of Ronan's psalmists in a single cast. He made another throw with the second spear at the cleric himself, so that it pierced the bell that hung from his neck, and the shaft sprang off into the air. Ronan burst out:

My curse fall on Sweeney
for his great offence.
His smooth spear profaned
my bell's holiness,

cracked bell hoarding grace
since the first saint rang it—
it will curse you to the trees,
bird-brain among branches.

Just as the spear-shaft broke
and sprang into the air
may the mad spasms strike
you, Sweeney, forever.

My fosterling lies slain,
your spear-point has been reddened:
to finish off this bargain
you shall die at spear-point.

Should the steadfast tribe of Owen
try to oppose me,
Uradhran and Telle
will visit them with decay.

Uradhran and Telle
have visited them with decay.
Until time dies away
my curse attend you.

My blessing on Eorann,
that she flourish and grow lovely.
Through everlasting pain
my curse fall on Sweeney.

There were three great shouts as the herded armies clashed
and roared out their war cries like stags. When Sweeney heard
these howls and echoes assumed into the travelling clouds and
amplified through the vaults of space, he looked up and he
was possessed by a dark rending energy.

His brain convulsed,
his mind split open.
Vertigo, hysteria, lurchings
and launchings came over him,
he staggered and flapped desperately,
he was revolted by the thought of known places
and dreamed strange migrations.
His fingers stiffened,
his feet scuffled and flurried,
his heart was startled,
his senses were mesmerized,
his sight was bent,
the weapons fell from his hands
and he levitated in a frantic cumbersome motion
like a bird of the air.
And Ronan's curse was fulfilled.

His feet skimmed over the grasses so lightly he never unsettled
a dewdrop and all that day he was a hurtling visitant of plain
and field, bare mountain and bog, thicket and marshland, and
there was no hill or hollow, no plantation or forest in Ireland
that he did not appear in that day; until he reached Ros
Bearaigh in Glen Arkin, where he hid in a yew tree in the glen.

13 Donal, son of Aodh, won the battle that day. A kinsman of
Sweeney's called Aongus the Stout survived and came fleeing
with a band of his people into Glen Arkin. They were won-
dering about Sweeney because they had not seen him alive
after the fight and he had not been counted among the
casualties. They were discussing this and deciding that Ronan's
curse had something to do with it when Sweeney spoke out
of the yew:

14
        Soldiers, come here.
        You are from Dal-Arie,
        and the man you are looking for
        roosts in his tree.

        The life God grants me now
        is bare and strait;
        I am haggard, womanless,
        and cut off from music.

        So I am here at Ros Bearaigh.
        Ronan has brought me low,
        God has exiled me from myself—
        soldiers, forget the man you knew.

15 When the men heard Sweeney's recitation they knew him at
once and tried to persuade him to trust them. He said he
never would, and as they closed round the tree, he launched
himself nimbly and lightly and flew to Kilreagan in Tyrconnell,
where he perched on the old tree by the church.
    It turned out that Donal, son of Aodh, and his army were

there after the battle, and when they saw the madman lighting in the tree, a crowd of them ringed and besieged it. They began shouting out guesses about the creature in the branches; one would say it was a woman, another that it was a man, until Donal himself recognized him and said:

—It is Sweeney, the king of Dal-Arie, the man that Ronan cursed on the day of the battle. That is a good man up there, he said, and if he wanted wealth and store he would be welcome to them, if only he would trust us. I am upset that Congal's people are reduced to this, for he and I had strong ties before we faced the battle. But then, Sweeney was warned by Colmcille when he went over with Congal to ask the king of Scotland for an army to field against me. Then Donal uttered the lay:

> Sweeney, what has happened here? 16
> Sweeney, who led hosts to war
> and was the flower among them all
> at Moira on that day of battle!
>
> To see you flushed after a feast,
> poppy in the gold of harvest.
> Hair like shavings or like down,
> your natural and perfect crown.
>
> To see your handsome person go
> was morning after a fall of snow.
> The blue and crystal of your eyes
> shone like deepening windswept ice.

Surefooted, elegant, except
you stumbled in the path of kingship,
you were a blooded swordsman, quick
to sense a chance and quick to strike.

Colmcille promised you, good son,
kingship and salvation:
how eagerly you strutted forth
blessed by that voice of heaven and earth.

Truthful seer, Colmcille
prophesied in this oracle:
All crossed the sea and here you stand
who'll never all return from Ireland.

Find the answer to his riddle
at Moira on the field of battle,
a gout of blood on a shining blade,
Congal Claon among the dead.

17 When Sweeney heard the shouts of the soldiers and the big
noise of the army, he rose out of the tree towards the dark
clouds and ranged far over mountains and territories.

A long time he went faring all through Ireland,
poking his way into hard rocky clefts,
shouldering through ivy bushes,
unsettling falls of pebbles in narrow defiles,
wading estuaries,

(1 2)

breasting summits,
trekking through glens,
until he found the pleasures of Glen Bolcain.

That place is a natural asylum where all the madmen of
Ireland used to assemble once their year in madness was
complete.

Glen Bolcain is like this:
it has four gaps to the wind,
pleasant woods, clean-banked wells,
cold springs and clear sandy streams
where green-topped watercress and languid brooklime
philander over the surface.
It is nature's pantry
with its sorrels, its wood-sorrels,
its berries, its wild garlic,
its black sloes and its brown acorns.

The madmen would beat each other for the pick of its water-
cresses and for the beds on its banks.

Sweeney stayed a long time in that glen until one night he 18
was cooped up in the top of a tall ivy-grown hawthorn. He
could hardly endure it, for every time he twisted or turned,
the thorny twigs would flail him so that he was prickled and
cut and bleeding all over. He changed from that station to
another one, a clump of thick briars with a single young
blackthorn standing up out of the thorny bed, and he settled

(1 3)

in the top of the blackthorn. But it was too slender. It wobbled and bent so that Sweeney fell heavily through the thicket and ended up on the ground like a man in a bloodbath. Then he gathered himself up, exhausted and beaten, and came out of the thicket, saying:

—It is hard to bear this life after the pleasant times I knew. And it has been like this a year to the night last night!

Then he spoke this poem:

19
A year until last night
I have lived among trees,
between flood and ebb-tide,
going cold and naked

with no pillow for my head,
no human company
and, so help me, God,
no spear and no sword!

No sweet talk with women.
Instead, I pine
for cresses, for clean
pickings of brooklime.

No surge of royal blood,
camped here in solitude;
no glory flames the wood,
no friends, no music.

Tell the truth: a hard lot.
And no shirking this fate;
no sleep, no respite,
no hope for a long time.

No house humming full,
no men, loud with good will,
nobody to call me king,
no drink or banqueting.

A great gulf yawns now
between me and that retinue,
between craziness and reason.
Scavenging through the glen

on my mad royal visit:
no pomp or king's circuit
but wild scuttles in the wood.
Heavenly saints! O Holy God!

No skilled musicians' cunning,
no soft discoursing women,
no open-handed giving;
my doom to be a long dying.

Far other than to-night,
far different my plight
the times when with firm hand
I ruled over a good land.

Prospering, smiled upon,
curbing some great steed,
I rode high, on the full tide
of good luck and kingship.

That tide has come and gone
and spewed me up in Glen Bolcain,
disabled now, outcast
for the way I sold my Christ,

fallen almost through death's door,
drained out, spiked and torn,
under a hard-twigged bush,
the brown, jaggy hawthorn.

Our sorrows were multiplied
that Tuesday when Congal fell.
Our dead made a great harvest,
our remnant, a last swathe.

This has been my plight.
Fallen from noble heights,
grieving and astray,
a year until last night.

20   He remained in that state in Glen Bolcain until at last he
mustered his strength and flew to Cloonkill on the borders of
Bannagh and Tyrconnell. That night he went to the edge of
the well for a drink of water and a bite of watercress and after
that he went into the old tree by the church. That was a very

bad night for Sweeney. There was a terrible storm and he despaired, saying:

—It is a pity I wasn't killed at Moira instead of having to put up with hardship like this.

Then he said this poem:

> To-night the snow is cold.
> I was at the end of my tether
> but hunger and bother
> are endless.
>
> Look at me, broken
> and down-at-heel,
> Sweeney from Rasharkin.
> Look at me now
>
> always shifting,
> making fresh pads,
> and always at night.
> At times I am afraid.
>
> In the grip of dread
> I would launch and sail
> beyond the known seas.
> I am the madman of Glen Bolcain,
>
> wind-scourged, stripped
> like a winter tree
> clad in black frost
> and frozen snow.

Hard grey branches
have torn my hands,
the skin of my feet
is in strips from briars

and the pain of frostbite
has put me astray,
from Slemish to Slieve Gullion,
from Slieve Gullion to Cooley.

I went raving with grief
on the top of Slieve Patrick,
from Glen Bolcain to Islay,
from Kintyre to Mourne.

I waken at dawn
with a fasting spittle:
then at Cloonkill, a bunch of cress,
at Kilnoo, the cuckoo flower.

I wish I lived safe
and sound in Rasharkin
and not here, heartbroken,
in my bare pelt, at bay in the snow.

22 Sweeney kept going until he reached the church at Swim-Two-Birds on the Shannon, which is now called Cloonburren; he arrived there on a Friday, to be exact. The clerics of the church were singing nones, women were beating flax

and one was giving birth to a child.

—It is unseemly, said Sweeney, for the women to violate the Lord's fast day. That woman beating the flax reminds me of our beating at Moira.

Then he heard the vesper bell ringing and said:

—It would be sweeter to listen to the notes of the cuckoos on the banks of the Bann than to the whinge of this bell to-night.

Then he uttered the poem:

I perched for rest and imagined   23
cuckoos calling across water,
the Bann cuckoo, calling sweeter
than church bells that whinge and grind.

Friday is the wrong day, woman,
for you to give birth to a son,
the day when Mad Sweeney fasts
for love of God, in penitence.

Do not just discount me. Listen.
At Moira my tribe was beaten,
beetled, heckled, hammered down,
like flax being scutched by these women.

From the cliff of Lough Diolar
to Derry Colmcille
I saw the great swans, heard their calls
sweetly rebuking wars and battles.

From lonely cliff-tops, the stag
bells and makes the whole glen shake
and re-echo. I am ravished.
Unearthly sweetness shakes my breast.

O Christ, the loving and the sinless,
hear my prayer, attend, O Christ,
and let nothing separate us.
Blend me forever in your sweetness.

24 The next day Sweeney went on to St. Derville's church, west
of Erris, where he fed on watercress and drank the water that
was in the church. The night was tempestuous, and he was
shaken with grief at his misery and deprivation. He was also
homesick for Dal-Arie and spoke these verses:

25   I pined the whole night
        in Derville's chapel
        for Dal-Arie
        and peopled the dark

        with a thousand ghosts.
        My dream restored me:
        the army lay at Drumfree
        and I came into my kingdom,

        camped with my troop,
        back with Faolchu and Congal
        for our night at Drumduff.
        Taunters, will-o'-the-wisps,

who saw me brought to heel
at Moira, you crowd my head
and fade away
and leave me to the night.

Sweeney wandered Ireland for all of the next seven years   26
until one night he arrived back in Glen Bolcain. That was
his ark and his Eden, where he would go to ground and
would only leave when terror struck. He stayed there that
night and the next morning Lynchseachan arrived looking
for him. Some say Lynchseachan was a half-brother of
Sweeney's, some say he was a foster-brother, but whichever
he was, he was deeply concerned for Sweeney and brought
him back three times out of his madness.

This time Lynchseachan was after him in the glen and
found his footprints on the bank of the stream where Sweeney
would go to eat watercress. He also followed the trail of
snapped branches where Sweeney had shifted from tree to
tree. But he did not catch up that day, so he went into a
deserted house in the glen and lay down, fatigued by all his
trailing and scouting. Soon he was in a deep sleep.

Then Sweeney, following the tracks of his tracker, was led
to the house and stood listening to the snores of Lynchseachan;
and consequently he came out with this poem:

I dare not sink down, snore and fall   27
fast asleep like the man at the wall,
I who never batted an eye
during the seven years since Moira.

(2 1)

God of Heaven! Why did I go
battling out that famous Tuesday
to end up changed into Mad Sweeney,
roosting alone up in the ivy?

From the well of Drum Cirb, watercress
supplies my bite and sup at terce;
its juices that have greened my chin
are Sweeney's markings and birth-stain.

And the manhunt is an expiation.
Mad Sweeney is on the run
and sleeps curled beneath a rag
under the shadow of Slieve League—

long cut off from the happy time
when I lived apart, an honoured name;
long exiled from those rushy hillsides,
far from my home among the reeds.

I give thanks to the King above
whose harshness only proves His love
which was outraged by my offence
and shaped my new shape for my sins—

a shape that flutters from the ivy
to shiver under a winter sky,
to go drenched in teems of rain
and crouch under thunderstorms.

Though I still have life, haunting deep
in the yew glen, climbing mountain slopes,
I would swop places with Congal Claon,
stretched on his back among the slain.

My life is steady lamentation
that the roof over my head has gone,
that I go in rags, starved and mad,
brought to this by the power of God.

It was sheer madness to imagine
any life outside Glen Bolcain—
Glen Bolcain, my pillow and heart's ease,
my Eden thick with apple trees.

What does he know, the man at the wall,
how Sweeney survived his downfall?
Going stooped through the long grass.
A sup of water. Watercress.

Summering where herons stalk.
Wintering out among wolf-packs.
Plumed in twigs that green and fall.
What does he know, the man at the wall?

I who once camped among mad friends
in Bolcain, that happy glen of winds
and wind-borne echoes, live miserable
beyond the dreams of the man at the wall.

28 After that poem he arrived, on the following night, at a mill owned by Lynchscachan. The caretaker of the mill was Lynchseachan's mother-in-law, an old woman called Lonnog, daughter of Dubh Dithribh. When Sweeney went in to see her she gave him a few scraps to eat and so, for a long time, he kept coming back to the mill.

One day when Lynchseachan was out trailing him, he caught sight of Sweeney by the mill-stream, and went to speak to the old woman.

—Has Sweeney come to the mill? said Lynchseachan.

—He was here last night, said the woman.

Lynchseachan then disguised himself as his mother-in-law and sat on in the mill after she had gone, until Sweeney arrived that night. But when Sweeney saw the eyes under the shawl, he recognized Lynchseachan and at once sprang out of his reach and up through the skylight, saying:

—This is a pitiful jaunt you are on, Lynchseachan, hunting me from every place I love in Ireland. Don't you know Ronan has left me with the fears of a bird, so I cannot trust you? I am exasperated at the way you are constantly after me.

And he made this poem:

29
> Lynchseachan, you are a bother.
> Leave me alone, give me peace.
> Is it not enough that Ronan doomed me
> to live furtive and suspicious?
>
> When I let fly that fatal spear
> at Ronan in the heat of battle

it split his holy breastplate open,
it dented his cleric's bell.

When I nailed him in the battle
with one magnificent spear-cast,
—Let the freedom of the birds be yours!
was how he prayed, Ronan the priest.

And I rebounded off his prayer
up, up and up, flying through air
lighter and nimbler and far higher
than I would ever fly again.

To see me in my morning glory
that Tuesday morning, turn time back;
still in my mind's eye I march out
in rank, in step with my own folk.

But now with my own eyes I see
something more miraculous even:
under the hood of a woman's shawl,
the shifty eyes of Lynchseachan.

—All you intend is to make me ridiculous, he said. Leave 30
off, harass me no more but go back to your own place and I
will go on to see Eorann.

When Sweeney deserted the kingship, his wife had gone to 31
live with Guaire. There had been two kinsmen with equal

rights to the kingship Sweeney had abandoned, two grand-
sons of Scannlan's called Guaire and Eochaidh. At that time,
Eorann was with Guaire and they had gone hunting through
the Fews towards Edenterriff in Cavan. His camp was near
Glen Bolcain, on a plain in the Armagh district.

Sweeney landed on the lintel of Eorann's hut and spoke
to her:

—Do you remember, lady, the great love we shared when
we were together? Life is still a pleasure to you but not to me.

And this exchange ensued between them:

32 *Sweeney*: Restless as wingbeats
of memory, I hover
above you, and your bed
still warm from your lover.

Remember when you played
the promise-game with me?
Sun and moon would have died
if ever you lost your Sweeney!

But you have broken trust,
unmade it like a bed—
not mine in the dawn frost
but yours, that he invaded.

Eorann: Welcome here, my crazy dote,
my first and last and favourite!
I am easy now, and yet I wasted
at the cruel news of your being bested.

Sweeney: There's more welcome for the prince
who preens for you and struts
to those amorous banquets
where Sweeney feasted once.

Eorann: All the same, I would prefer
a hollow tree and Sweeney bare—
that sweetest game we used to play—
to banqueting with him to-day.

I tell you, Sweeney, if I were given
the pick of all in earth and Ireland
I'd rather go with you, live sinless
and sup on water and watercress.

Sweeney: But cold and hard as stone
lies Sweeney's path
through the beds of Lisardowlin.
There I go to earth

in panic, starved and bare,
a rickle of skin and bones.
I am yours no longer.
And you are another man's.

Eorann: My poor tormented lunatic!
When I see you like this it makes me sick,
your cheek gone pale, your skin all scars,
ripped and scored by thorns and briars.

Sweeney: And yet I hold no grudge,
       my gentle one.
       Christ ordained my bondage
       and exhaustion.

Eorann: I wish we could fly away together,
       be rolling stones, birds of a feather:
       I'd swoop to pleasure you in flight
       and huddle close on the roost at night.

Sweeney: I have gone north and south.
       One night I was in the Mournes.
       I have wandered as far as the Bann mouth
       and Kilsooney.

33 They had no sooner finished than the army swept into the camp from every side, and as usual, he was away in a panic, never stopping until twilight, when he arrived at Ros Bearaigh —that church where he first halted after the battle of Moira— and again he went into the yew tree of the church. Murtagh McEarca was erenach of the church at the time and his wife was passing the yew when by chance she caught sight of the madman. Recognizing Sweeney, she said:

—Come down out of the yew. I know you are king of Dal-Arie, and there is nobody here but myself, a woman on her own.

That is what she said, though she hoped to beguile him somehow into a trap and catch him.

—Indeed I shall not come down, said Sweeney, for Lynchseachan and his wife might come upon me. But am I not hard to recognize nowadays?

And he uttered these stanzas:

> Only your hawk eye 34
> could pick me out
> who was cock of the walk once
> in Dal-Arie—
>
> the talk of Ireland
> for looks and bearing.
> Since the shock of battle
> I'm a ghost of myself.
>
> So mind your husband
> and your house, good woman,
> but I can't stay. We shall meet again
> on Judgement Day.

He cleared the tree lightly and nimbly and went on his way 35 until he reached the old tree in Rasharkin, which was one of the three hide-outs he had in his own country, the others being at Teach mic Ninnedha and Cluan Creamha. He lodged undiscovered there for six weeks in the yew tree but he was detected in the end and the nobles of Dal-Arie held a meeting to decide who should go to apprehend him. Lynchseachan was the unanimous choice and he agreed to go.

Off he went to the tree and Sweeney was there, perched on a branch above him.

—It is a pity, Sweeney, he said, that you ended up like this, like any bird of the air, without food or drink or clothes, you that went in silk and satin and rode foreign steeds in their matchless harness. Do you remember your train, the lovely gentle women, the many young men and their hounds, the retinue of craftsmen? Do you remember the assemblies under your sway? Do you remember the cups and goblets and carved horns that flowed with pleasant heady drink? It is a pity to find you like any poor bird flitting from one waste ground to the next.

—Stop now, said Sweeney, it was my destiny. But have you any news for me about my country?

—I have indeed, said Lynchseachan, for your father is dead.

—That is a seizure, he said.

—Your mother is dead too, said the young man.

—There'll be pity from nobody now, he said.

—And your brother, said Lynchseachan.

—My side bleeds for that, said Sweeney.

—Your daughter is dead, said Lynchseachan.

—The heart's needle is an only daughter, said Sweeney.

—And your son who used to call you daddy, said Lynchseachan.

—Indeed, he said, that is the drop that fells me to the ground.

After that, Sweeney and Lynchseachan made up this poem between them:

36 *Lynchseachan*: Sweeney from the high mountains,
blooded swordsman, veteran:
for Christ's sake, your judge and saviour,
speak to me, your foster-brother.

If you hear me, listen. Listen,
my royal lord, my great prince,
for I bring you, gently as I can,
bad news from your homeland.

You left behind a dead kingdom.
Therefore I had to come
with tidings of a dead brother,
a father dead, a dead mother.

Sweeney: If my gentle mother's dead, I face
a harder exile from my place;
yet she had cooled in love of me
and love that's cooled is worse than pity.

The son whose father's lately dead
kicks the trace and lives unbridled.
His pain's a branch bowed down with nuts.
A dead brother is a wounded side.

Lynchseachan: Things the world already knows
I still must break to you as news:
thin as you are, and bare, your wife
pined after you, and died of grief.

Sweeney: A household when the wife is gone,
a boat that's rudderless in storm;
it is pens of feathers next the skin;
a widower at his bleak kindling.

Lynchseachan: Sorrow accumulates: heartbreak,
keenings, wailings fill the air.
But all of it's a fist round smoke
now you are without a sister.

Sweeney: No common wisdom I invoke
can stanch the wound made by that stroke.
A sister's love is still, unselfish,
like sunlight mild upon a ditch.

Lynchseachan: Our north is colder than it was,
calves are kept in from their cows
since your daughter and sister's son,
who both loved you, were stricken down.

Sweeney: My faithful hound, my faithful nephew—
no bribe could buy their love of me.
But you've unstitched the rent of sorrow.
The heart's needle is an only daughter.

Lynchseachan: This telling what I would keep back
wounds me to the very quick!
In Dal-Arie, everyone
mourns the death of your son.

Sweeney: Ah! Now the gallows trap has opened
that drops the strongest to the ground!
A haunted father's memory
of his small boy calling *Daddy*!

This is a blow I cannot stand.
This sorrow is the one command
I must obey. His death fells me,
defenceless, harmless, out of the tree.

Lynchseachan: Sweeney, now you are in my hands,
I can heal these father's wounds:
your family has fed no grave,
all your people are alive.

Calm yourself. Come to. Rest.
Come home east. Forget the west.
Admit, Sweeney, you have come far
from where your heart's affections are.

Woods and forests and wild deer,
now these things delight you more
than sleeping in your eastern dun
on a bed of feather down.

Near a quick mill-pond, your perch
on a dark green holly branch
means more to you than any feast
among the brightest and the best.

Harp music in the breasting hills
would not soothe you: you would still
strain to hear from the oak-wood
the brown stag belling to the herd.

Swifter than the wind in glens,
once the figure of a champion,
a legend now, and a madman—
your exile's over, Sweeney. Come.

37   When Sweeney heard the news of his only son he fell from the yew tree and Lynchseachan caught him and put manacles on him. Then he told him that all his people were alive, and escorted him back to the assembled nobles of Dal-Arie. They produced locks and fetters in which they shackled Sweeney and left him under Lynchseachan's supervision for the next six weeks. During that time the nobles of the province kept visiting him, and at the end of it, his sense and memory came back to him and he felt himself restored to his old shape and manner. So they took the tackle off him and he was back to his former self, the man they had known as king.

After that, Sweeney was quartered in Lynchseachan's bedroom. Then harvest time came round and one day Lynchseachan went with his people to reap. Sweeney, shut in the bedroom, was left in the care of the mill-hag, who was warned not to speak to him. All the same, she did speak to him, asking him to relate some of his adventures when he was in his state of madness.

—A curse on your mouth, hag, said Sweeney, for your talk is dangerous. God will not allow me to go mad again.

—It was your insult to Ronan that put you mad, said the hag.

—This is hateful, he said, to have to put up with your treachery and trickery.

—It is no treachery, only the truth.

And Sweeney said:

Sweeney: Hag, did you come here from your mill   38
       to spring me over wood and hill?
       Is it to be a woman's ploy
       and treachery send me astray?

The Hag: Sweeney, your sorrows are well known,
       and I am not the treacherous one:
       the miracles of holy Ronan
       maddened and drove you among madmen.

Sweeney: If I were king and I wish I were
       again the king who held sway here,
       instead of the banquet and ale-mug
       I'd give you a fist on the mouth, hag.

—Now listen, woman, he said, if you only knew the hard 39
times I have been through. Many's the dreadful leap I have
leaped from hill and fort and land and valley.

—For God's sake, said the hag, let me see one of those
leaps now. Show me how you did it when you were off in
your madness.

With that, he bounded over the bed-rail and lit on the end
of the bench.

—Sure I could do that leap myself, said the hag, and she
did it.

Then Sweeney took another leap out through the skylight
of the lodge.

—I could do that too, said the hag, and leaped it, there
and then.

Anyhow, this is the way it ended up: Sweeney went lifting over five cantreds of Dal-Arie that day until he arrived at Gleann na n-Eachtach in Feegile and she was on his heels the whole way. When he took a rest there, in the top of an ivy-bunch, the hag perched on another tree beside him.

It was the end of the harvest season and Sweeney heard a hunting-call from a company in the skirts of the wood.

—This will be the outcry of the Ui Faolain coming to kill me, he said. I slew their king at Moira and this host is out to avenge him.

He heard the stag bellowing and he made a poem in which he praised aloud all the trees of Ireland, and rehearsed some of his own hardships and sorrows, saying:

40

Suddenly this bleating
and belling in the glen!
The little timorous stag
like a scared musician

startles my heartstrings
with high homesick refrains—
deer on my lost mountains,
flocks out on the plain.

The bushy leafy oak tree
is highest in the wood,
the forking shoots of hazel
hide sweet hazel-nuts.

The alder is my darling,
all thornless in the gap,
some milk of human kindness
coursing in its sap.

The blackthorn is a jaggy creel
stippled with dark sloes;
green watercress in thatch on wells
where the drinking blackbird goes.

Sweetest of the leafy stalks,
the vetches strew the pathway;
the oyster-grass is my delight,
and the wild strawberry.

Low-set clumps of apple trees
drum down fruit when shaken;
scarlet berries clot like blood
on mountain rowan.

Briars curl in sideways,
arch a stickle back,
draw blood and curl up innocent
to sneak the next attack.

The yew tree in each churchyard
wraps night in its dark hood.
Ivy is a shadowy
genius of the wood.

Holly rears its windbreak,
a door in winter's face;
life-blood on a spear-shaft
darkens the grain of ash.

Birch tree, smooth and blessed,
delicious to the breeze,
high twigs plait and crown it
the queen of trees.

The aspen pales
and whispers, hesitates:
a thousand frightened scuts
race in its leaves.

But what disturbs me most
in the leafy wood
is the to and fro and to and fro
of an oak rod.

Ronan was dishonoured,
he rang his cleric's bell:
my spasm and outrage
brought curse and miracle.

And noble Congal's armour,
his tunic edged in gold,
swathed me in doomed glory
with omens in each fold.

His lovely tunic marked me
in the middle of the rout,
the host pursuing, shouting:
—The one in the gold coat.

Get him, take him live or dead,
every man fall to.
Draw and quarter, pike
and spit him, none will blame you.

Still the horsemen followed
across the north of Down,
my back escaping nimbly
from every javelin thrown.

As if I had been cast
by a spearsman, I flew high,
my course a whisper in the air,
a breeze flicking through ivy.

I overtook the startled fawn,
kept step with his fleet step,
I caught, I rode him lightly—
from peak to peak we leapt,

mountain after mountain,
a high demented spree
from Inishowen south,
and south, as far as Galtee.

From Galtee up to Liffey
I was swept along and driven
on through bitter twilight
to the slopes of Benn Bulben.

And that was the first night
of my long restless vigil:
my last night at rest,
the eve of Congal's battle.

And then Glen Bolcain was my lair,
my earth and den;
I've scaled and strained against those slopes
by star and moon.

I wouldn't swop a lonely hut
in that dear glen
for a world of moorland acres
on a russet mountain.

Its water flashing like wet grass,
its wind so keen,
its tall brooklime, its watercress
the greenest green.

I love the ancient ivy tree,
the pale-leafed sallow,
the birch's whispered melody,
the solemn yew.

And you, Lynchseachan, can try
disguise, deceit;
come in the mask and shawl of night,
I won't be caught.

You managed it the first time
with your litany of the dead:
father, mother, daughter, son,
brother, wife—you lied

but if you want your say again,
then be ready
to face the heights and crags of Mourne
to follow me.

I would live happy
in an ivy bush
high in some twisted tree
and never come out.

The skylarks rising
to their high space
send me pitching and tripping
over stumps on the moor

and my hurry flushes
the turtle-dove.
I overtake it,
my plumage rushing,

am startled
by the startled woodcock
or a blackbird's sudden
volubility.

Think of my alarms,
my coming to earth
where the fox still
gnaws at the bones,

my wild career
as the wolf from the wood
goes tearing ahead
and I lift towards the mountain,

the bark of foxes
echoing below me,
the wolves behind me
howling and rending—

their vapoury tongues,
their low-slung speed
shaken off like nightmare
at the foot of the slope.

If I show my heels
I am hobbled by guilt.
I am a sheep
without a fold

who sleeps his sound sleep
in the old tree at Kilnoo,
dreaming back the good days
with Congal in Antrim.

A starry frost will come
dropping on pools
and I'll be astray here
on unsheltered heights:

herons calling
in cold Glenelly,
flocks of birds quickly
coming and going.

I prefer the elusive
rhapsody of blackbirds
to the garrulous blather
of men and women.

I prefer the squeal of badgers
in their sett
to the tally-ho
of the morning hunt.

I prefer the re-
echoing belling of a stag
among the peaks
to that arrogant horn.

Those unharnessed runners
from glen to glen!
Nobody tames
that royal blood,

each one aloof
on its rightful summit,
antlered, watchful.
Imagine them,

the stag of high Slieve Felim,
the stag of the steep Fews,
the stag of Duhallow, the stag of Orrery,
the fierce stag of Killarney.

The stag of Islandmagee, Larne's stag,
the stag of Moylinny,
the stag of Cooley, the stag of Cunghill,
the stag of the two-peaked Burren.

The mother of this herd
is old and grey,
the stags that follow her
are branchy, many-tined.

I would be cloaked in the grey
sanctuary of her head,
I would roost among
her mazy antlers

and would be lofted into
this thicket of horns
on the stag that lows at me
over the glen.

I am Sweeney, the whinger,
the scuttler in the valley.
But call me, instead,
Peak-pate, Stag-head.

The springs I always liked
were the fountain at Dunmall
and the spring-well on Knocklayde
that tasted pure and cool.

Forever mendicant,
my rags all frayed and scanty,
high in the mountains
like a crazed, frost-bitten sentry

I find no bed nor quarter,
no easy place in the sun—
not even in this reddening
covert of tall fern.

My only rest: eternal
sleep in holy ground
when Moling's earth lets fall
its dark balm on my wound.

But now that sudden bleating
and belling in the glen!
I am a timorous stag
feathered by Ronan Finn.

41 After that poem, Sweeney went on from Feegile through
Bannagh, Benevenagh and Maghera but he could not shake
off the hag until he reached Dunseverick in Ulster. There he
leaped from the summit of the fort, down a sheer drop, coax-
ing the hag to follow. She leaped quickly after him but fell
on the cliff of Dunseverick, where she was smashed to pieces
and scattered into the sea. That is how she got her end on
Sweeney's trail.

42 Then Sweeney said:
    —From now on, I won't tarry in Dal-Arie because Lynch-
seachan would have my life to avenge the hag's.
    So he proceeded to Roscommon in Connacht, where he
alighted on the bank of the well and treated himself to water-
cress and water. But when a woman came out of the erenach's
house, he panicked and fled, and she gathered the watercress
from the stream. Sweeney watched her from his tree and
greatly lamented the theft of his patch of cress, saying:
    —It is a shame that you are taking my watercress. If only
you knew my plight, how I am unpitied by tribesman or kins-
man, how I am no longer a guest in any house on the ridge
of the world. Watercress is my wealth, water is my wine, and
hard bare trees and soft tree bowers are my friends. Even if

you left that cress, you would not be left wanting; but if you take it, you are taking the bite from my mouth.

And he made this poem:

> Woman, picking the watercress
> and scooping up my drink of water,
> were you to leave them as my due
> you would still be none the poorer.
>
> Woman, have consideration,
> we two go two different ways:
> I perch out among tree-tops,
> you lodge here in a friendly house.
>
> Woman, have consideration.
> Think of me in the sharp wind,
> forgotten, past consideration,
> without a cloak to wrap me in.
>
> Woman, you cannot start to know
> sorrows Sweeney has forgotten:
> how friends were so long denied him
> he killed his gift for friendship even.
>
> Fugitive, deserted, mocked
> by memories of my days as king,
> no longer called to head the troop
> when warriors are mustering,

43

no longer the honoured guest
at tables anywhere in Ireland,
ranging like a mad pilgrim
over rock-peaks on the mountain.

The harper who harped me to rest,
where is his soothing music now?
My people too, my kith and kin,
where did their affection go?

In my heyday, on horseback,
I rode high into my own:
now memory's an unbroken horse
that rears and suddenly throws me down.

Over starlit moors and plains,
woman plucking my watercress,
to his cold and lonely station
the shadow of that Sweeney goes

with watercress for his herds
and cold water for his mead,
bushes for companions,
the bare hillside for his bed.

Hugging these, my cold comforts,
still hungering after cress,
above the bare plain of Emly
I hear cries of the wild geese,

and still bowed to my hard yoke,
still a bag of skin and bone,
I reel as if a blow hit me
and fly off at the cry of a heron

to land maybe in Dairbre
in spring, when days are on the turn,
to scare away again by twilight
westward, into the Mournes.

Gazing down at clean gravel,
to lean out over a cool well,
drink a mouthful of sunlit water
and gather cress by the handful—

even this you would pluck from me,
lean pickings that have thinned my blood
and chilled me on the cold uplands,
hunkering low when winds spring up.

Morning wind is the coldest wind,
it flays me of my rags, it freezes—
the very memory leaves me speechless,
woman, picking the watercress.

Woman: *Judge not and you won't be judged.*
Sweeney, be kind, learn the lesson
that vengeance belongs to the Lord
and mercy multiplies our blessings.

Sweeney: Then here is justice, fair and even,
from my high court in the yew:
Leave the patch of cress for me,
I shall give my rags in lieu.

I have no place to lay my head.
Human love has failed me. So
let me swop sins for watercress,
let thieving make a scapegoat of you.

Your greed has left me hungering
so may these weeds you robbed me of
come between you and good luck
and leave you hungering for love.

As you snatched cress, may you be snatched
by the foraging, blue-coated Norse.
And live eaten by remorse.
And cursing God that our paths crossed.

44 He stayed in Roscommon that night and the next day he
went on to Slieve Aughty, from there to the pleasant slopes
of Slemish, then on to the high peaks of Slieve Bloom, and
from there to Inishmurray. After that, he stayed six weeks in
a cave that belonged to Donnan on the island of Eig off the
west of Scotland. From there he went on to Ailsa Craig, where
he spent another six weeks, and when he finally left there he
bade the place farewell and bewailed his state, like this:

Without bed or board
I face dark days
in frozen lairs
and wind-driven snow.

Ice scoured by winds.
Watery shadows from weak sun.
Shelter from the one tree
on a plateau.

Haunting deer-paths,
enduring rain,
first-footing the grey
frosted grass.

I climb towards the pass
and the stag's belling
rings off the wood,
surf-noise rises

where I go, heartbroken
and worn out,
sharp-haunched Sweeney,
raving and moaning.

The sough of the winter night,
my feet packing the hailstones
as I pad the dappled
banks of Mourne

or lie, unslept, in a wet bed
on the hills by Lough Erne,
tensed for first light
and an early start.

Skimming the waves
at Dunseverick,
listening to billows
at Dun Rodairce,

hurtling from that great wave
to the wave running
in tidal Barrow,
one night in hard Dun Cernan,

the next among the wild flowers
of Benn Boirne;
and then a stone pillow
on the screes of Croagh Patrick.

I shift restlessly
on the plain of Boroma,
from Benn Iughoine
to Benn Boghaine.

Then that woman
interfered,
disturbed me
and affronted me

and made off with
the bite from my mouth.
It is constant,
this retribution,

as I gather cress
in tender bunches,
four round handfuls
in Glen Bolcain,

and unpick
the shy bog-berry,
then drink water
from Ronan's well.

My nails are bent,
my loins weak,
my feet bleeding,
my thighs bare—

I'll be overtaken
by a stubborn band
of Ulstermen
faring through Scotland.

But to have ended up
lamenting here
on Ailsa Craig.
A hard station!

Ailsa Craig,
the seagulls' home,
God knows it is
hard lodgings.

Ailsa Craig,
bell-shaped rock,
reaching sky-high,
snout in the sea—

it hard-beaked,
me seasoned and scraggy:
we mated like a couple
of hard-shanked cranes.

I tread the slop
and foam of beds,
unlooked for,
penitential,

and imagine treelines
somewhere beyond,
a banked-up, soothing,
wooded haze,

not like the swung
depths and swells
of that nightmare-black
lough in Mourne.

I need woods
for consolation,
some grove in Meath—
or the space of Ossory.

Or Ulster in harvest.
Strangford, shimmering.
Or a summer visit
to green Tyrone.

At Lammas I migrate
to the springs of Teltown,
pass the spring fishing
the bends of the Shannon.

I often get as far
as my old domain,
those groomed armies,
those stern hillsides.

Then Sweeney left Ailsa Craig and flew over the stormy maw 46
of the sea to the land of the Britons. He passed their royal
stronghold on his right and discovered a great wood where he
could hear wailing and lamentation. Sometimes it was a great
moan of anguish, sometimes an exhausted sigh. The moaner
turned out to be another madman astray in the wood. Sweeney
approached him.

—Who are you, friend? Sweeney asked.
—A madman, said he.

—In that case, you are a friend indeed. I am a madman myself, said Sweeney. Why don't you join up with me?

—I would, the other man said, except that I am in dread of the king or the king's retinue capturing me, and I am not sure that you are not one of them.

—I am no such thing, said Sweeney, and since you can trust me, tell me your name.

—They call me the Man of the Wood, said the madman.

Then Sweeney spoke this verse and the Man of the Wood answered as follows:

47 *Sweeney*: What happened, Man of the Wood,
         to make you whinge
         and hobble like this? Why did
         your mind unhinge?

   Man: Caution and fear of the king
         have silenced me.
         I made a tombstone of my tongue
         to keep my story.

         I am the Man of the Wood.
         I was famous
         in battles once. Now I hide
         among bushes.

Sweeney: I come from the Bush myself.
         I am Sweeney,
         son of Colman. Like yourself,
         outcast, shifty.

After that, they did confide in each other and shared their life
stories. Sweeney said to the madman:

—Tell me about yourself.

—I am a landowner's son, said the mad Briton, a native of
this country, and my name is Alan.

—Tell me, Sweeney asked, what made you mad?

—It is simple. Once upon a time there were two kings in
this country, struggling for the kingship. Their names were
Eochaidh and Cuagu. Eochaidh was the better king and I
am one of his people. Anyhow, the issue was to be decided at
a great muster where there was to be a battle. I laid solemn
obligations on each of my chief's people that none was to
come to the battle unless he was arrayed in silk. I did this so
that they would be magnificent, outstanding beyond the
others in pomp and panoply. But, for doing that, the hosts
cursed me with three howls of malediction that sent me astray
and frightened, the way you see me.

In the same way he asked Sweeney what drove him to madness.

—The words of Ronan, said Sweeney. At the battle of
Moira he cursed me in front of the armies so that I sprang out
of the battle and have been wandering and fleeing ever since.

—O Sweeney, said Alan, since we have trusted each other,
let us now be guardians to each other.

> Whoever of us is the first to hear
> the cry of a heron from a lough's blue-green waters
> or the clear note of a cormorant
> or the flight of a woodcock off a branch

or the wheep of a plover disturbed in its sleep
or the crackle of feet in withered branches,
or whoever of us is the first to see
the shadow of a bird above the wood,
let him warn the other.
Let us move always
with the breadth of two trees between us.
And if one of us hears any of these things
or anything like them,
let both of us scatter immediately.

50 So they went about like that for a year. At the end of the
year Alan said to Sweeney:

—To-day is the day we must part, for the end of my life has
come, and I will go where I am destined to meet my death.

—How will you die? Sweeney asked.

—That is simple, Alan said. I will proceed now to the
waterfall at Doovey, where a blast of wind will unbalance
me and pitch me into the waterfall, so that I'll be drowned.
Afterwards, I will be buried in the churchyard of a saint.
And I'll go to heaven. And now, Sweeney, said Alan, tell me
what your own fate will be.

Sweeney told him what this story goes on to tell and they
parted. The Briton set out for the waterfall and when he
reached it he was drowned in it.

51 Then Sweeney came to Ireland, reaching the plain of Moy-
linny, in Antrim, as the evening was drawing on. When he
realized where he was, he said:

—This was always a good plain, and I was here once with a

good man. That was Scannlan's son, my friend Congal Claon. One day here I said to Congal that I wanted to go to another lord and master because the rewards I got from him were too small. To persuade me to stay with him, Congal immediately gave me a hundred and fifty lovely horses, and his own brown steed into the bargain; and a hundred and fifty flashing swords, hafted in tusks; fifty servants and fifty servant girls; a tunic made of cloth-of-gold, and a magnificent girdle of chequered silk.

Then Sweeney recited this poem:

Now my bare skin feels 52
night falling on Moylinny,
the plain where Congal lived.
Now in my memory

I see Congal and me
riding across the plain
deep in conversation,
headed for Drum Lurgan.

I am saying to the king:
—The services I give
are not being rewarded.
And I threaten I will leave.

What does the king do then?
He gives me in their hundreds
horses, bridles, swords, foreign
captives, girl attendants.

And my great chestnut steed,
the best that grazed or galloped,
his cloth-of-gold tunic,
his girdle of silk plaits.

So what plain matches this plain?
Is it the plain of Meath
or the plain of Airgeadros
or Moyfevin with its crosses?

Moylurg or Moyfea,
the lovely plain of Connacht,
the Liffey banks, Bannside,
or the plain of Muirhevna?

I have seen all of them,
north, south, east, and west,
but never saw the equal
of this ground in Antrim.

53 When he had made that poem Sweeney came on to Glen
Bolcain, where he went wandering freely until he met with a
madwoman. He shied and ran away from her, yet divining
somehow that she too was simple-minded, he stopped in his
tracks and turned to her. With that, she shied and ran away
from him.

—Alas, God, Sweeney said, life is a misery. I scare away
from her and she scares away from me. And in Glen Bolcain,
of all places!

Then he began:

(6 0)

Whoever stirs up enmity should never have been born;
may every bitter man and woman
be barred at the gate of heaven.

If three conspire and combine
one will backbite or complain
as I complain, going torn
by briar and sharp blackthorn.

First, madwoman flees from man.
Then, something stranger even:
barefoot, in his bare skin,
man runs away from woman.

In November, wild ducks fly.
From those dark days until May
let us forage, nest and hide
in ivy in the brown wood

and hear behind birds' singing
water sounds in Glen Bolcain,
its fast streams, all hush and jabber,
its islands on forking rivers,

its hazel trees and holly bowers,
its acorns and leaves and briars,
its nuts, its sharp-tasting sloes,
its sweet, cool-fleshed berries:

(6 1)

and under trees, its hounds coursing,
its loud stags bellowing,
its waters' clear endless fall—
what enmity is possible?

55 After that, Sweeney went to the house where his wife, Eorann,
was lodging with her retinue of maidservants. He stood at the
outer door of the house and spoke to his former queen:

—Here you are, Eorann, laid in the lap of luxury, and still
there is no lap for me to lie in.

—That is how it is, Eorann said, but do come in.

—Indeed I will not, said Sweeney, in case the army traps
me in the house.

—Well, said the woman, it seems your mind has not got
any better, and since you do not want to stop with us, why
don't you go away and leave us in peace? There are people
here who knew you when you were in your right mind; it
would be an embarrassment if they were to see you like this.

—Isn't that terrible, said Sweeney. Now I know it. It is
fatal to trust a woman. And I was generous to this one. She
is spurning me now but I would have been the man of the
moment if I had come back that day when I slew Oilill
Caedach, the king of Ui Faolain.

And with that he said:

56 Any man a woman falls for,
however handsome, should beware.
Mad Sweeney is the proof,
cast off by his first love.

And any trusting man must stay
on guard for their treachery
because betrayal like Eorann's
is second nature in a woman.

Gullible and open-handed,
straightforward, wide-eyed,
I gave steeds and herds away,
filled her pastures in a day.

In the thick of fighting men
I could more than hold my own:
when the battle cry was sounded
I handled thirty single-handed.

It was Congal's right to ask for
a warrior to champion Ulster:
—Who among you will take on
the fighter king of Ui Faolain?

Oilill was a berserk giant,
a shield and spear in either hand,
so overbearing in his stride
for a while our ranks were daunted.

But when I spoke at Congal's side
it was not to whinge or backslide:
—Though Oilill is their strongest bastion,
I will hold the line against him.

I left him shortened by a head
and left the torso, overjoyed,
and left five other princes dead
before I stopped to wipe my blade.

57 With that, Sweeney rose lightly and stealthily and went
hopping airily from peak to peak, from one hill to the next,
until he reached Mourne in the south of Ulster. He rested
there, saying:

—This is a good place for a madman, but it is no place for
corn or milk or food. And though it is a lovely, lofty station,
it is still uncomfortable and uneasy. There is no shelter here
from the storm or the shower.

And then he uttered these words:

58
The Mournes are cold to-night,
my station is desolate:
no milk or honey in this land
of snowfields, gusting wind.

In a sharp-branched holly tree,
exhausted, nothing on me,
chilled to the bone, every night
I camp on the mountain summit.

Frost casts me like an effigy
unless I shift and break free
when gales from the plain of Leinster
fan me alive, a bleak ember

dreaming, when summer dies
round Hallowe'en and All-Hallows,
another move to my old ground—
the clear springs of Glen Bolcain.

Astray no more east or west,
blizzards whipping my bare face,
not shivering in some drifted den,
a starved, pinched, raving madman,

but sheltered in that lovely glen,
my winter harbour, my haven,
my refuge from the bare heath,
my royal fort, my king's rath.

All night there I glean and raid
and forage in the oak wood.
My hands feel out leaf and rind,
roots, windfalls on the ground,

they comb through matted watercress
and grope among the bog-berries,
brooklime, sorrel, damp moss,
wild garlic, raspberries,

apples, hazel-nuts, acorns,
haws of the sharp, jaggy hawthorn,
and blackberries, floating weed,
the whole store of the oak wood.

> Keep me here, Christ, far away
> from open ground and flat country.
> Let me suffer the cold of glens.
> I dread the cold space of plains.

59 The next morning Sweeney started again. He passed Moyfevin and the clear, green-wavering Shannon; he passed the inviting slopes of Aughty, the spreading pastures of Loughrea, the delightful banks of the River Suck, and landed on the shores of broad Lough Ree. He spent that night in the fork of Bile Tiobradain, which was one of his favourite hide-outs in the country. It was Creegaille, in the east of Connacht.

Great sorrow and misery descended on him and he said:

—Indeed I have suffered great trouble and distress. It was cold in the Mournes last night and it is no better to-night in the fork of Bile Tiobradain.

60 It was snowing that night, and as fast as the snow fell, it was frozen. So he said:

—I have endured purgatories since the feathers grew on me. And still there is no respite. I realize, he said, that even if it were to mean my death, it would be better to trust my people than to endure these woes forever.

Then he recited the poem, proclaiming aloud his woes:

61
> Almighty God, I deserved this,
> my cut feet, my drained face,
> winnowed by a sheer wind
> and miserable in my mind.

Last night I lay in Mourne
plastered in wet; cold rain poured.
To-night, in torment, in Glasgally
I am crucified in the fork of a tree.

I who endured unflinchingly
through long nights and long days
since the feathers penned my frame
foresee nothing but the same.

Hard weather has withered me,
blizzards have buried me.
As I wince here in cutting wind
Glen Bolcain's heather haunts my mind.

Unsettled, panicky, astray,
I course over the whole country
from Liffey to Lower Bann,
from Bannside to the banks of Lagan;

then over Rathmore to Roscommon,
and fields that lie around Cruachan,
above Moylurg's level plain
and the brow of bushy Fews Mountain.

Or else I make a tough migration
to the Knockmealdown mountains;
or from Glasgally, a long glide
eastward to a louth hillside.

All this is hard to thole, Lord!
Still without bed or board,
crouching to graze on cress,
drinking cold water from rivers.

Alarmed out of the autumn wood,
whipped by whins, flecked with blood,
running wild among wolf-packs,
shying away with the red stag.

Son of God, have mercy on us!
Never to hear a human voice!
To sleep naked every night
up there in the highest thickets,

to have lost my proper shape and looks,
a mad scuttler on mountain peaks,
a derelict doomed to loneliness:
Son of God, have mercy on us!

62 —All the same, Sweeney said, even if Donal, son of Aodh,
were to kill me, I will still go to Dal-Arie and trust to the
mercy of my own people. If the mill-hag had not duped me
into that bout of leaping, I would still be sane enough.

63 Then a glimmer of reason came back to him and he set out
for his own country, ready to settle there and entrust himself
to the people.

Ronan heard of Sweeney's return to his senses and his
decision to go back among his own, and cried out:

—I beseech you, Lord, that the persecutor may not come near the church to torment it again; I beseech you, do not relent in your vengeance or ease his affliction until he is sundered body from soul in his death-swoon. Remember that you struck him for an example, a warning to tyrants that you and your people were sacred and not to be lightly dishonoured or outraged.

God answered Ronan's prayer. When Sweeney was out on the 64 uplands of the Fews he halted, stalk still: a strange apparition rose before him at midnight. Bleeding headless torsos and disembodied heads—five scraggy, goat-bearded heads— screamed and bounced this way and that over the road. When he got among them, they were talking to each other.
   —He is a madman, said the first head.
   —A madman from Ulster, said the second.
   —Follow him well, said the third.
   —May the pursuit be long, said the fourth.
   —Until he reaches the sea, said the fifth.
   They rose in a flock, coming for him, but he soared away in front, skimming from thicket to thicket; and no matter how wide the glen that opened before him, he bounded from edge to edge, from the top of one hill to the top of the next.

> The heads were pursuing him,   65
> lolling and baying,
> snapping and yelping,
> whining and squealing.

They nosed at his calves and his thighs,
they breathed on his shoulder,
they nuzzled the back of his neck,
they went bumping off tree-trunks and rock-face,
they spouted and plunged like a waterfall,
until he gave them the slip and escaped
in a swirling tongue of low cloud.

66 He had lost them, goat-head and dog-head and the whole
terrifying pack he had sensed there. But his previous wandering and flying were nothing compared with what he suffered
now, for he was startled into a fit which lasted six weeks until
he perched one night in the top of a tree, on the summit of
Slieve Eidhneach. In the morning he began lamenting:

67   My dark night has come round again.
            The world goes on but I return
            to haunt myself. I freeze and burn.
            I am the bare figure of pain.

            Frost crystals and level ice,
            the scourging snow, the male-voiced storm
            assist at my requiem.
            My hearth goes cold, my fire dies.

            Are there still some who call me prince?
            The King of Kings, the Lord of All
            revoked my title, worked my downfall,
            unhoused, unwived me for my sins.

Why did He spare my life at Moira?
Why did He grudge me death in battle?
Why ordained the hag of the mill
His hound of heaven and my fury?

The mill-hag's millstone round my neck!
Hell roast her soul! She dragged me down
when I leaped up in agitation.
I fell for that old witch's trick.

Then Lynchseachan was in full cry,
a bloodhound never off my trail.
I fell for his lies too and fell
among captors out of the tree.

They made me face the love I'd lost.
They tied me up and carried me
back to the house. The mockery!
I overheard their victory feast

yet gradually grew self-possessed,
for there were decent people there,
and gaming and constant laughter.
My mind was knitting up at last

but soon unravelled into nightmare.
I was for the high jump once more.
The mill-hag spun her web and swore
her innocence. I leaped for her

and leaped beyond the bounds of sense.
She challenged me a second time.
We kept in step like words in rhyme.
I set the pace and led the dance—

I cleared the skylight and the roof,
I flew away beyond the fortress
but she hung on. Through smooth and rough
I raised the wind and led the chase.

We coursed all over Ireland then.
I was the wind and she was smoke.
I was the prow and she the wake.
I was the earth and she the moon.

But always look before you leap!
Though she was fit for bog and hill,
Dunseverick gave her the spill.
She followed me down off the top

of the fort and spread-eagled
her bitch's body in the air.
I trod the water, watching her
hit the rocks. And I was glad

to see her float in smithereens.
A crew of devils made a corpse
of her and buried it. Cursed
be the ground that housed her bones.

One night I walked across the Fews—
the hills were dark, the starlight dead—
when suddenly five severed heads,
five lantern ghouls, appeared and rose

like bats from hell, surrounding me.
Then a head spoke—another shock!
—This is the Ulster lunatic.
Let us drive him into the sea.

I went like an arrow from a bow.
My feet disdained that upland ground.
Goat-head and dog-head cursed but found
me impossible to follow.

I have deserved all this:
night-vigils, terror,
flittings across water,
women's cried-out eyes.

One time during his wild career Sweeney left Slieve Lougher 68
and landed in Feegile. He stayed there for a year among the
clear streams and branches of the wood, eating red holly-
berries and dark brown acorns, and drinking from the River
Feegile. At the end of that time, deep grief and sorrow
settled over him because of his terrible life; so he came out
with this short poem:

69   Look at Sweeney now, alas!
His body mortified and numb,
unconsoled, sleepless
in the rough blast of the storm.

From Slieve Lougher I came
to the border marches of Feegile,
my diet still the usual
ivy-berries and oak-mast.

I have spent a year on the mountain
enduring my transformation,
dabbing, dabbing like a bird
at the holly-berries' crimson.

My grief is raw and constant.
To-night all my strength is gone.
Who has more cause to lament
than Mad Sweeney of Glen Bolcain?

70 One day Sweeney went to Drum Iarann in Connacht where
he stole some watercress and drank from a green-flecked well.
A cleric came out of the church, full of indignation and re-
sentment, calling Sweeney a well-fed, contented madman,
and reproaching him where he cowered in the yew tree:

71   *Cleric*: Aren't you the contented one?
You eat my watercress,
then you perch in the yew tree
beside my little house.

Sweeney: Contented's not the word!
          I am so terrified,
          so panicky, so haunted
          I dare not bat an eyelid.

          The flight of a small wren
          scares me as much, bell-man,
          as a great expedition
          out to hunt me down.

          Were you in my place, monk,
          and I in yours, think:
          would you enjoy being mad?
          Would you be contented?

Once when Sweeney was rambling and raking through Con-   72
nacht he ended up in Alternan in Tireragh. A community of
holy people had made their home there, and it was a lovely
valley, with a turbulent river shooting down the cliff; trees
fruited and blossomed on the cliff-face; there were sheltering
ivies and heavy-topped orchards, there were wild deer and
hares and fat swine; and sleek seals, that used to sleep on the
cliff, having come in from the ocean beyond. Sweeney coveted
the place mightily and sang its praises aloud in this poem:

          Sainted cliff at Alternan,   73
          nut grove, hazel-wood!
          Cold quick sweeps of water
          fall down the cliff-side.

Ivies green and thicken there,
its oak-mast is precious.
Fruited branches nod and bend
from heavy-headed apple trees.

Badgers make their setts there
and swift hares have their form;
and seals' heads swim the ocean,
cobbling the running foam.

And by the waterfall, Colman's son,
haggard, spent, frost-bitten Sweeney,
Ronan of Drumgesh's victim,
is sleeping at the foot of a tree.

74 At last Sweeney arrived where Moling lived, the place that is
known as St. Mullins. Just then, Moling was addressing him-
self to Kevin's psalter and reading from it to his students.
Sweeney presented himself at the brink of the well and began
to eat watercress.

    —Aren't you the early bird? said the cleric; and continued,
with Sweeney answering, as follows:

75   *Moling*: So, you would steal a march on us,
                up and breakfasting so early!
   Sweeney: Not so very early, priest.
                Terce has come in Rome already.

Moling: And what knowledge has a fool
about the hour of terce in Rome?
Sweeney: The Lord makes me His oracle
from sunrise till sun's going down.

Moling: Then speak to us of hidden things,
give us tidings of the Lord.
Sweeney: Not I. But if you are Moling,
you are gifted with the Word.

Moling: Mad as you are, you are sharp-witted.
How do you know my face and name?
Sweeney: In my days astray I rested
in this enclosure many a time.

Moling: But Sweeney, son of Colman Cuar,
why won't you settle in one place?
Sweeney: The resting place that I prefer
is life in everlasting peace.

Moling: God help you then. Do you not dread
the slippery brim of hell's wide mouth?
Sweeney: My one affliction is that God
denies me repose on earth.

Moling: Come closer. Come here and share
whatever morsels you would like.
Sweeney: There are worse things, priest, than hunger.
Imagine living without a cloak.

Moling: Then you are welcome to my smock,
and welcome to take my cowl.
Sweeney: Sometimes memory brings back
times it hurts me to recall.

Moling: Are you Sweeney, the bogey-man,
escaped out of the fight at Moira?
Sweeney: I am the early bird, the one
who scavenges, if I am Sweeney.

Moling: Mad as you are, how does it come
you were fit to recognize me?
Sweeney: In this enclosure many times
I watched you from a far eyrie.

Moling: Look at this leaf of Kevin's book,
the coilings on this psalter's page.
Sweeney: The yew leaf coils around my nook
in Glen Bolcain's foliage.

Moling: This churchyard, this flush of colour,
is there no pleasure here for you?
Sweeney: My pleasure is great and other:
the hosting that day at Moira.

Moling: I will sing Mass, make a hush
of high celebration.
Sweeney: Leaping an ivy bush
is a higher calling even.

Moling: My ministry is only toil,
the weak and strong both exhaust me.
Sweeney: I toil to a bed on the chill
steeps of Benevenagh.

Moling: When your end comes, will it be
death by water, in holy ground?
Sweeney: It will be early when I die.
One of your herds will make the wound.

—You are more than welcome here, Sweeney, said Moling, 76
for you are fated to live and die here. You shall leave the his-
tory of your adventures with us and receive a Christian burial
in a churchyard. Therefore, said Moling, no matter how far
you range over Ireland, day by day, I bind you to return to me
every evening so that I may record your story.

All during the next year the madman kept coming back to 77
Moling. One day he would go to Inishbofin in west Connacht,
another day to lovely Assaroe. Some days he would view the
clean lines of Slemish, some days he would be shivering on the
Mournes. But wherever he went, every night he would be back
for vespers at St. Mullins.

Moling ordered his cook to leave aside some of each day's
milking for Sweeney's supper. This cook's name was Muirghil
and she was married to a swineherd of Moling's called Mon-
gan. Anyhow, Sweeney's supper was like this: she would sink
her heel to the ankle in the nearest cow-dung and fill the hole
to the brim with new milk. Then Sweeney would sneak into
the deserted corner of the milking yard and lap it up.

(7 9)

78 One night there was a row between Muirghil and another woman, in the course of which the woman said:

—If you do not prefer your husband, it is a pity you cannot take up with some other man than the looney you have been meeting all year.

The herd's sister was within earshot and listening but she said nothing until the next morning. Then when she saw Muirghil going to leave the milk in the cow-dung beside the hedge where Sweeney roosted, she came in to her brother and said:

—Are you a man at all? Your wife's in the hedge yonder with another man.

Jealousy shook him like a brainstorm. He got up in a sudden fury, seized a spear from a rack in the house, and made for the madman. Sweeney was down swilling the milk out of the cow-dung with his side exposed towards the herd, who let go at him with the spear. It went into Sweeney at the nipple of his left breast, went through him, and broke his back.

There is another story. Some say the herd had hidden a deer's horn at the spot where Sweeney drank from the cow-dung and that Sweeney fell and killed himself on the point of it.

79 Enna McBracken was ringing the bell for prime at the door of the churchyard and saw what had happened. He spoke this poem:

80   This is sad, herd, this was deliberate,
             outrageous, sickening and sinful.

Whoever struck here will live to regret
killing the king, the saint, the holy fool.

What good did you expect to come of it?
Repentance will be denied you at your death.
Your soul will go howling to the devil,
your body draw an unabsolved last breath.

But I expect to be with him in heaven,
united in a single strain of prayer.
The soul of the true guest is sped by psalms
on the lips of a fasting, chanting choir.

My heart is breaking with pity for him.
He was a man of fame and high birth.
He was a king, he was a madman.
His grave will be a hallowing of earth.

Enna went back and told Moling that Sweeney had been 81
killed by his swineherd Mongan. Immediately, Moling and
his community came along to where Sweeney lay and Sweeney
repented and made his confession to Moling. He received
Christ's body and thanked God for having received it and
after that was anointed by the clerics.

Sweeney: There was a time when I preferred   83
            the turtle-dove's soft jubilation
            as it flitted round a pool
            to the murmur of conversation.

There was a time when I preferred
the blackbird singing on the hill
and the stag loud against the storm
to the clinking tongue of this bell.

There was a time when I preferred
the mountain grouse crying at dawn
to the voice and closeness
of a beautiful woman.

There was a time when I preferred
wolf-packs yelping and howling
to the sheepish voice of a cleric
bleating out plainsong.

You are welcome to pledge healths
and carouse in your drinking dens;
I will dip and steal water
from a well with my open palm.

You are welcome to that cloistered hush
of your students' conversation;
I will study the pure chant
of hounds baying in Glen Bolcain.

You are welcome to your salt meat
and fresh meat in feasting-houses;
I will live content elsewhere
on tufts of green watercress.

The herd's sharp spear wounded me
and passed clean through my body.
Ah Christ, who disposed all things, why
was I not killed at Moira?

Of all the innocent lairs I made
the length and breadth of Ireland
I remember an open bed
above the lough in Mourne.

Of all the innocent lairs I made
the length and breadth of Ireland
I remember bedding down
above the wood in Glen Bolcain.

To you, Christ, I give thanks
for your Body in communion.
Whatever evil I have done
in this world, I repent.

Then Sweeney's death-swoon came over him and Moling, 84
attended by his clerics, rose up and each of them placed a
stone on Sweeney's grave.

—The man who is buried here was cherished indeed, said
Moling. How happy we were when we walked and talked
along this path. And how I loved to watch him yonder at the
well. It is called the Madman's Well because he would often
eat its watercress and drink its water, and so it is named after
him. And every other place he used to haunt will be cherished,
too.

And then Moling said:

I am standing beside Sweeney's tomb
remembering him. Wherever he
migrated in flight from home
will always be dear to me.

Because Sweeney loved Glen Bolcain
I learned to love it, too. He'll miss
the fresh streams tumbling down,
the green beds of watercress.

He would drink his sup of water from
the well yonder we have called
the Madman's Well; now his name
keeps brimming in its sandy cold.

I waited long but knew he'd come.
I welcomed, sped him as a guest.
With holy viaticum
I limed him for the Holy Ghost.

Because Sweeney was a pilgrim
to the stoup of every well
and every green-frilled, cress-topped stream,
their water's his memorial.

Now, if it be the will of God,
rise, Sweeney, take this guiding hand

that has to lay you in the sod
and draw the dark blinds of the ground.

I ask a blessing, by Sweeney's grave.
His memory flutters in my breast.
His soul roosts in the tree of love.
His body sinks in its clay nest.

After that, Sweeney rose out of his swoon. Moling took him 86
by the hand and both went towards the door of the church.
When they reached the door Sweeney leaned his shoulders
against the jamb and breathed a loud sigh. His spirit fled to
heaven and his body was given an honourable burial by
Moling.

These have been some of the stories about the adventures of 87
Sweeney, son of Colman Cuar, king of Dal-Arie.